More Jokes for Children

MORE JOKES
for
CHILDREN

by

MARGUERITE KOHL
FREDERICA YOUNG

Illustrated by Bob Patterson

REVISED EDITION

ᗝ HILL AND WANG • NEW YORK

A division of Farrar, Straus and Giroux

Printed in the United States of America

Quality Printing and Binding by:
R.R. Donnelley & Sons Company
1009 Sloan Street
Crawfordsville, IN 47933 U.S.A.

0-374-45360-8

FOREWORD

This collection of jokes was written for children and inspired by them. As an elementary-school teacher, I have discovered even the non-reader will read a joke book. Quiet as well as active children are eager to share the latest riddle or knock-knock with friends. I'm right there to enjoy their wonderful enthusiasm and happy smiles.

Thanks, kids!

FREDERICA YOUNG
March 1984

CONTENTS

CONTENTS

More Jokes for Children

Conundrums (Riddles)

What's the difference between a cat and a match?
A cat lights on its feet and a match lights on its head.

Where was King Solomon's temple?
On the side of his head.

What part of London is in France?
The letter *n*.

What are people called who ride on Greyhound buses?
Passengers.

What is the best thing to take when you are run down?
The license plate of the car that hit you.

What is the difference between a pill and a hill?
One's hard to get down, the other is hard to get up.

Is there any word in the English language that contains all the vowels?

Unquestionably.

What has a big mouth and can't talk?
A jar.

Why did the girl eat bullets?
Because she wanted to grow bangs.

Why did the man go off the side of the cliff with his truck?
He wanted to test his air brakes.

Why doesn't the corn like the farmer?
Because he picks his ears.

Why is a cat longer at night than in the morning?
They let him out at night and they bring him in in the morning.

What trees are left behind after a fire?
Ashes.

What book contains more stirring pages than any other?
A cook book.

Why is a pencil like a riddle?
It's no good without a point.

What did Ringo Starr say when he fell off a cliff?
"I want to hold your hand."

What has no arms, no legs or feet, and climbs very high?
Fire.

What has four eyes and can't see?
The Mississippi.

When are cooks mean?
When they beat the eggs and whip the cream.

Which is the left side of a pie?
The side that isn't eaten.

What has a mouth but doesn't speak and a bed it doesn't sleep in?
A river.

Why can't it rain for two days in a row?
Because there's a night in between.

How do you make seven even?
Take off the s.

Which burns longer, a short candle, a long candle, or a chubby candle?
None of them. They all burn shorter.

Why did people start night baseball?
Because bats like to sleep in the daytime.

Why is a half-moon heavier than a full moon?
A full moon is lighter.

What is the oldest piece of furniture in the world?
The multiplication table.

What can you serve but not eat?
A ping-pong ball.

Why should a horse never be hungry on a journey?
It always has a bit in its mouth.

What begins with *p*, ends with *e*, and has more than two hundred letters in it?

A post office.

What's the most-used letter in the alphabet?
E because it's in everything.

Why did the two hairs say good-by?
Because they knew they would soon be parted.

What smells most in a flower shop?
Your nose.

Why didn't they play cards on Noah's Ark?
Because Noah sat on the deck.

What has a bark but no bite?
A tree.

What did the tie say to the hat?
"You go on ahead while I hang around."

What head does not have a brain in it?
A nailhead.

Why was the wheel the greatest thing ever invented?
Because it started things rolling.

What has a hand but can't scratch itself?
A clock.

What room can no one enter?
A mushroom.

What is the only thing you can break when you say its name?
Silence.

What roof never keeps out the wet?
The roof of your mouth.

Why does the ocean get angry?
Because it's been crossed so many times.

What kind of clothing lasts the longest?
Underwear, because it is never worn out.

What man can raise things without lifting them?
A farmer.

What kind of shoes are made of banana skins?
Slippers.

Why is there no such thing as a whole day?
Because every morning the day breaks.

Why are you like two people when you lose your temper?
You are beside yourself.

What has neither flesh nor bone, but has four fingers and
a thumb?
A glove.

The more you take away, the bigger it gets—what is it?
A hole.

Which travels faster, heat or cold?
Heat, because you can easily catch cold.

Why are dentists such sad persons?
They're always looking down in the mouth.

What goes through a door but never comes in or goes out?
A keyhole.

On what side of a church does an oak tree grow?
The outside.

Why is an island like the letter *t*?
Because it is in the middle of water.

What is the smallest bridge in the world?
The bridge of your nose.

What has three feet but cannot walk?
A yard.

What can you hold without touching it?
Your breath.

If there were twenty dogs running after one dog, what time would it be?

Twenty after one.

What did one wall say to the other?
"Meet you at the corner."

Why did the man throw a clock out the window?
He wanted to see time fly.

What has a stone but can't throw it?
A peach.

What's black and white and dangerous?
A poisoned black and white cooky.

Who is the only man you always take your hat off to?
The barber.

Why do they name hurricanes after girls?
If they named them after boys, they would be called himicanes.

What has an arm but can't raise it?
A chair.

A penny and a dollar were on a table. The penny jumped off, why didn't the dollar?

The dollar had more sense.

How do you make soup gold?
You put in fourteen carrots.

What is a volcano?
A mountain with hiccups.

What is white, has a horn, and gives milk?
A milk truck.

What ten-letter word starts with gas?
Automobile.

What did the bald man say when he got a comb for a gift?
"I'll never part with it."

Have you heard about the new doctor doll?
You wind it up and it operates on batteries.

What does a librarian use for bait when she goes fishing?
Bookworms.

Why is a packed baseball field always cool?
It has fans in every seat.

What's purple and flies?
Supergrape.

What is too much for one, just right for two, but nothing at all for three?
A secret.

What is the highest building in town?
The library because it has the most stories.

On which side of a pitcher is the handle?
The outside.

What is black, sits in a tree, and is very dangerous?
A crow with a machine gun.

What has four legs and one foot?
A bed.

Where was the first doughnut made?
In Greece.

Give me two reasons for some people not minding their own business?
1. No mind
2. No business

What wears shoes but has no feet?
The sidewalk.

Why is a duke like a book?
Because he has a title.

What falls and doesn't break?
Night falls and day breaks.

When is an artist unhappy?
When he draws a long face.

What falls in winter but never gets hurt?
Snow.

What is noisier than a pig in a sty?
Two pigs in a sty.

What is the difference between a talkative girl and an umbrella?
You can shut the umbrella up.

What is small, purple, and dangerous?
A grape with a machine gun.

What stays in bed and runs south?
The Mississippi River.

When is an egg like a losing team?
When it is being beaten.

Why is Sunday the strongest day of the week?
Because all the other days are weekdays.

When is a little girl's dress like a frog?
When it's a jumper.

What's always behind the time?
The back of a clock.

Why is a calendar so sad?
Because its days are numbered.

When is a tree like a woman's coat?
When it's a fir.

Why is a clock like a river?
Neither runs very long without winding.

When did the river overflow its banks?
When it got too big for its bridges.

What can speak all the languages of the world?
An echo.

What did the dirt say when it rained?
"If this keeps up, my name is mud."

What is taken before you get it?
Your picture.

Why does a bald-headed man have no use for keys?
He has lost his locks.

What keeps a magazine alive?
A good circulation.

Why is a man on an island like a lady?
They're both looking for a sale.

When is a piece of wood like a king?
When it's a ruler.

Why is the sun able to stay up in the sky?
Because it has so many beams.

What bus crossed the ocean?
Columbus.

What has a head, a tail, and no body?
A penny.

When will a net hold water?
When the water turns to ice.

Where did Noah strike the first nail in the Ark?
On the head.

Why Do They Call Him?

Why do they call him Ace?
Because he's such a card.

Why do they call him Mumps?
Because he's a swell guy.

Why do they call him Belt?
Because he gets around.

Why do they call him Birdseed?
Because he fills the bill.

Why do they call him Sip?
Because he has so many ups and downs.

Why do they call him Sunny?
Because he's such a bright boy.

Why do they call him Ruler?
Because he measures up.

Why do they call him Ball?
Because he's full of bounce.

Why do they call him Sugar?
Because he's so refined.

Why do they call him Hash?
Because he's a mixture of everything.

Why do they call him Finger?
Because he's thumb kid.

Why do they call him Beefy?
Because he's in his prime.

Signs Seen

Seen during a drought:
>Don't be a drip
>Save every drop

Sign in a restaurant window:
>Don't stand outside and be miserable,
>Come inside and be fed up!

Sign on a building:
>Wanted—woman to sew buttons on the third floor.

Sign on a men's store window:
> Fifteen men's wool suits, $15.00.
> They won't last an hour.

Sign on a roadside billboard:
> Hardly a soul is still alive
> Who passed on a hill at 75.

Advertising billboard:
> Big cattle show.
> Go over, see the show, meet your friends.

Sign in the window of an apartment house:
> Piano lessons.
> Special pains given to beginners.

Sign flashed on a movie screen:
A $50.00 bill has been found in the theatre. Will the owner please form a line at the box office?

Sign in a bakery window:
Cream puffs—6 for 29¢. The flakiest, puffiest of puffs crammed full of creamy mustard. Treat the family.

Sign in a candy factory:
> Help wanted, mechanic in candy factory
> to tighten the nuts in peanut brittle.

Sign at a road intersection:
>   Cross Road—Better Humor It.

Sign in a bait and tackle shop:
>   Worms with fish appeal.

Sign on a turnpike:
>   Drive right so more people will be left.

Sign at gas station:
>   There's a new gas
>   that puts a rabbit in your tank;
>   it's for short hops.

Sign on a dairy truck:
>   You can't beat our milk,
>   but you can whip our cream.

Sign in a store window:
> Why go elsewhere to be cheated
> when you can come here?

Sign on a highway:
> Take notice—when this sign
> is under water, this road is impassable.

Sign in a store:
> If our peanuts were any fresher,
> they'd be insulting.

Sign on sales lot for mobile homes:
> Wheel Estate.

Sign over goldfish display:
> Wet pets.

Sign on a delicatessen store wall:
> Our best is none too good.

Sign in a drugstore window:
> Don't fight a cold.
> That's what makes a cold sore.

Sign in front of a house:
> Anyone's welcome to use our lawn mower,
> if he doesn't take it out of our yard.

Double Talk

Why is Ireland rich?
Its capital is always Dublin.

I'm making metric cookies.
What are you going to call them?

Gram crackers.

What did E.T.'s mother say to him when he got home?
Where on earth have you been?

I have to go to the fruit market because my shoes are torn.
Why the fruit market?
So I can get another pair (pear).

What did Rudolf say to his wife on Christmas Eve?
"I hope it doesn't rain, dear."

What's the difference between a fish and a piano?
You can't tuna fish.

What continent do you see when you look in the mirror
in the morning?

Europe (you're up).

What do you get when you cross a baseball player with a
Boy Scout?

A boy who likes to pitch tents.

MAN TO TELEPHONE OPERATOR: Why can't you get me the
zoo?
OPERATOR: The lion is busy.

How can you tell this is a dogwood tree?
By its bark.

Do you know what the beaver said to the Christmas tree?
"It's been nice gnawing you."

Why did the man sleep under the oil tank?
He wanted to get up oily in the morning.

What puts the white lines on the ocean?
An ocean liner.

What Roman numeral can you make climb a wall?
I V

Have you any stage experience?
Yes, my leg was in a cast once.

Why is the word "farewell" like a bargain?
It's a good buy.

Did you hear the rope joke?
No.
Skip it!

Why did the baker stop baking doughnuts?
He got tired of the hole business.

What is the worst month for soldiers?
A long March.

Why was the little shoe so unhappy?

Because his mother was a sneaker and his father was a loafer.

Why did the basketball wear a bib?
So it wouldn't dribble.

How do you like being a chimney sweep?
It soots me.

When is a blow on the head like a piece of fabric?
When it is felt.

What did one daisy say to the other daisy?
"Take me to your weeder."

Can February march?
No, but April may.

EGYPTIAN: Who was that lady I saw you with last night?
FRIEND: That was no lady, that was my mummy.

Have you tried Beatle soap?
Put it in the tub and watch the ring go.

What did the rake say to the hoe?
"Hi, hoe!"

MAN: Didn't you tell me this would be a good steak?
WAITER: Yes, sir.
MAN: Well, it was a bum steer.

What is a prickly pear?
Two porcupines.

What kind of children does a stupid florist have?
Blooming idiots.

What do you call a frightened skin diver?
Chicken of the sea.

What is a hot chocolate?
Stolen candy.

What is a lumberjack?
A wooden pancake.

What did one penny say to the other penny?
"Let's get together and make some cents."

FIRST SALESMAN: My job is selling salt.
SECOND SALESMAN: That's my job too!
FIRST SALESMAN: Shake!

What did the ocean say to the plane that flew across it?
Nothing—it just waved.

I dreamed about a crippled polka-dotted horse last night.
It was a nightmare!

Did you hear about the Texas cowboy?

He bought a dachshund because someone told him to "get
a long little doggy."

Did you hear about the fight on the train?
The conductor punched a ticket.

If the Marines and the Navy were playing basketball and all the Marines fouled out, whom would they put in?

The submarines.

This is Miss Warner Cracker.
Which Miss Warner Cracker?
Polly Warner Cracker.

What do stars do when they get hungry?
They take a bite of Milky Way.

If you were walking down the street and smashed your toe, what would you do?

Call a tow truck.

Why is tennis such a noisy game?
Because each player raises a racket.

Are you going to take the car out in this rainstorm?
Certainly, it's a driving rain, isn't it?

Why did the man hit the log with a hammer?
Because he wanted a bump on a log.

Hello, this is Mr. Deggs.
Which Mr. Deggs?
Mr. Hammond Deggs.

PILOT: Do you wanta fly?
BOY: Sure!
PILOT: Wait a minute, I'll catch one for you.

TRAVELER: May I have a ticket to the moon?
AGENT: Sorry, the moon is full now.

ESCAPED PRISONER: Hurrah! I'm free! I'm free!
LITTLE BOY: So what! I'm four!

Barney and Benny

BARNEY: I guess I'll be going now. Don't trouble to see
me to the door.
BENNY: It's no trouble, it's a pleasure.

BENNY IN ART CLASS: Why did they hang my picture?
BARNEY: Must be because they couldn't find you.

BENNY: She's a smart girl. She has brains enough for two.
BARNEY: Then she's just the girl for you.

BARNEY: Are you trying to make a monkey out of me?
BENNY: Why should I take the credit?

BENNY: This soup isn't fit for a pig.
BARNEY: I'll take it back and bring you some that is.

BARNEY: Who's that terribly ugly man sitting over there?
BENNY: That's my brother.
BARNEY: Oh, I beg your pardon. I hadn't noticed the resemblance.

BENNY: What's yellow and green and eats grass?
BARNEY: What?
BENNY: A yellow and green grass-eater. What's yellow and blue and eats grass?
BARNEY: A yellow and blue grass-eater?
BENNY: Nope, they only come in yellow and green.

BARNEY: I have an unusual dog—he has no nose.
BENNY: How does he smell?
BARNEY: Awful!

BENNY: What looks like an Indian but isn't an Indian?
BARNEY: What?
BENNY: A picture of an Indian.

BARNEY: What's the difference between a loaf of bread and an elephant?

BENNY: I don't know.

BARNEY: Well, if you don't know the difference, I'm not sending you to the store for a loaf of bread.

BENNY: I keep seeing spots before my eyes.

BARNEY: Have you seen a doctor?

BENNY: No, just spots.

BARNEY: I just saw something running across the room with no legs.

BENNY: What was it?

BARNEY: Spilled milk.

BENNY: If I were gone for two years would you know me?

BARNEY: Yes.

BENNY: For ten years?

BARNEY: Yes.

BENNY: For twenty years?

BARNEY: Yes.

BENNY: Knock, knock.

BARNEY: Who's there?

BENNY: You forgot me already.

BARNEY: What are you taking for your cold?
BENNY: I don't know—how much will you give me?

BENNY: A banana truck weighed one ton, the bananas weighed 350 pounds, the first man on the truck weighed 160 pounds. What did the second man weigh?
BARNEY: I don't know.
BENNY: He weighed the bananas.

BARNEY: Name two different ways of saying "today" without saying "today."
BENNY: The day before tomorrow and the day after yesterday.

BARNEY: Why is winter the best time to buy thermometers?
BENNY: In the summer they're a lot higher.

BENNY: Why is the policeman the strongest man in town?
BARNEY: He can hold up the traffic with one hand.

BARNEY: There was only one match, and there was a candle, the fireplace, and a cigarette to be lighted. What should be lighted first?
BENNY: The match.

BENNY: Why is it bad to write on an empty stomach?
BARNEY: Paper is better.

BARNEY: I dropped a full glass and didn't spill a drop of
water.
BENNY: How come?
BARNEY: It was full of milk.

BENNY: TV will never take the place of newspapers.
BARNEY: Why?
BENNY: You can't start a fire with a TV set.

BARNEY: If you fell into the water, what would be the first
thing you'd do?
BENNY: Get wet.

BENNY: This match won't light.
BARNEY: What's the matter with it?
BENNY: I don't know, it worked a minute ago.

BARNEY: Why aren't you working?
BENNY: The boss and I had a fight and he won't take back
what he said.
BARNEY: What did he say?
BENNY: "You're fired!"

BENNY: I was in hot water last night.
BARNEY: What happened?
BENNY: I took a bath.

BENNY: Did you hear about the carpenter who drove a nail through his thumb? Now he has a thumbnail.

BARNEY: When does a brook stop running downhill?
BENNY: When it gets to the bottom.

BENNY: What should you do if you split your sides laughing?
BARNEY: Run until you get a stitch in them.

BARNEY: If you fed a cow money, what would you get?
BENNY: Rich milk.

BENNY: When they take your appendix out, it is an appendectomy. When they remove your tonsils, it is a tonsillectomy. What is it when they remove a growth from your head?
BARNEY: A haircut!

BARNEY: I didn't sleep so well last night.
BENNY: Why, what happened?
BARNEY: I plugged the electric blanket into the toaster by mistake and kept popping out of bed all night.

BENNY: Did you ever hear the joke about the ceiling?
BARNEY: No.
BENNY: I didn't think so. It's over your head.

BARNEY: What is the last thing you take off when you go to bed?
BENNY: You take your feet off the floor.

BENNY: What is the best way to make a fire with two sticks?
BARNEY: Make sure one of the sticks is a match.

BARNEY: Where does Thursday come before Wednesday?
BENNY: In the dictionary.

BARNEY: I can tell you the score of any baseball game just before it starts.
BENNY: What is it?
BARNEY: Nothing to nothing.

BENNY: I hear you had quite a cold spell in Florida.
BARNEY: Yes indeed, we were selling frozen orange juice right off the trees.

BARNEY: I know a man who drove a stagecoach and it didn't have any wheels.
BENNY: Yeah? What held it up?
BARNEY: Bandits.

BENNY: What's the best thing to put in a pie?
BARNEY: Your teeth.

BARNEY: What letter is not in the alphabet?
BENNY: The letter I put in the mailbox.

BENNY: Ever had any accidents?
BARNEY: Nope.
BENNY: Not ever?
BARNEY: No, but a dog bit me once.
BENNY: Well, don't you call that an accident?
BARNEY: Naw, he bit me on purpose.

BARNEY: That candy you're eating looks good.
BENNY: It is good.
BARNEY: It makes my mouth water.
BENNY: Well, here's a blotter.

BENNY: Do you know I have X-ray eyes?
BARNEY: No—what can you see through?
BENNY: Glass!

BENNY: I can be sick for nothing because my father is a doctor.

BARNEY: So what? I can be good for nothing because my father is a minister.

BARNEY: How long is the longest finger in the world?

BENNY: I don't know, how long?

BARNEY: Eleven inches. If it were twelve inches it would be a foot.

BENNY: If two is company and three's a crowd, what are four and five?

BARNEY: I don't know, what?

BENNY: Nine.

BENNY: What happened to your hand?

BARNEY: I put it into the horse's mouth to see how many teeth it had.

BENNY: Yeah?

BARNEY: And the horse closed its mouth to see how many fingers I had.

BENNY: Could you light a candle if you had a box of candles and no matches?

BARNEY: No.

BENNY: Yes, you could. Just take a candle out of the box and you'll make the box a candle lighter.

BARNEY: This liniment makes my arm smart.

BENNY: Why don't you rub some on your head!

BENNY: The other day I was looking for a book. All of a sudden I stopped.
DARNEY: Why?
BENNY: I found it.

BARNEY: Benny, your hair is getting thin.
BENNY: So what! Who wants fat hair?

BENNY: My father's in the hospital.
BARNEY: What's wrong with him?
BENNY: Nothing. He's a doctor.

BARNEY: Did you hear about the fellow who brushed his teeth with gunpowder?
BENNY: What happened?
BARNEY: He spent the rest of the day shooting off his mouth.

BENNY: There was something wrong with the meat I ate.
BARNEY: How do you know?
BENNY: I've got inside information.

BENNY: Do you know what a true friend is?
BARNEY: Sure. Someone who says nasty things to your face instead of saying them behind your back.

Rhymes—
with and without Reason

Jack and Jill went up the hill
To fetch a pail of water.
Jack fell down and broke his crown,
And Jill collapsed with laughter.

There was a small girl from Duluth
Who said, "I have broken a tooth!"
The dentist looked in
And said with a grin,
"T'ain't broken—it's just a bit loose."

It has a great trunk
That needs no key.
And a big rough bark,
But it won't bite me.
What is it? A tree.

As a rule, man is a fool.
When it's hot, he wants it cool.
When it's cool, he wants it hot,
Always wanting what is not.

The porcupine may have his quills,
The elephant his trunk,
But when it comes to common scents,
My money's on the skunk.

A fool does never change his mind,
And who can think it strange?
The reason's clear, for fools, my friends,
Have not a mind to change.

You can always tell the English,
You can always tell the Dutch,
You can always tell the Yankees,
But you can't tell them much!

Ooey Gooey was a worm,
A little worm was he.
He sat upon the railroad tracks,
The train he did not see.
Ooey, Gooey!

Long ago there was a cat,
Who swallowed a ball of yarn,
And when the cat had kittens,
They all had sweaters on.

He who stops to look each way,
Will drive his car another day.
But he who speeds across the "Stop"
Will land in the mortician's shop.

He rocked the boat,
Did Ezra Shank.
These bubbles mark

O
　O
　　O
　　　　Where Ezra sank.

I sneezed a sneeze into the air,
It fell to earth I know not where,
But hard and cold were the looks of those,
In whose vicinity I snooze.

Don't worry if your job is small,
And your rewards are few.
Remember that the mighty oak,
Was once a nut like you.

A doctor fell into a well
And broke his collarbone.
A doctor should attend the sick,
And leave the well alone.

Willie saw some dynamite,
Couldn't understand it quite,
But curiosity never pays—
It rained Willie seven days.

There was a young man from the city,
Who met what he thought was a kitty.
He gave it a pat,
And said, "Nice pussycat,"
And they buried his clothes out of pity.

There was a young fellow named Wier,
Who hadn't an atom of fear.
He indulged a desire
To touch a live wire—
(Most any last line will do here!)

There was a young fellow from Leeds,
Who swallowed six packets of seeds.
When a month came to pass,
He was covered with grass,
And he couldn't sit down for the weeds.

A peanut was sitting on a railroad track.
His heart was all a-flutter.
A train came running down the track—
Toot! Toot! Peanut butter.

There was a lady named May,
Who was always happy and gay.
But one day she was mad,
And then she grew sad—
What was wrong with her she wouldn't say.

There was an old man from Blackheath,
Who sat on his set of false teeth.
He cried with a start,
"Oh my, bless my heart,
I've bitten myself underneath."

There was a young fellow named Hall,
Who fell in the spring in the fall.
'Twould have been a sad thing
If he died in the spring,
But he didn't, he died in the fall.

There was an old man from Peru,
Who dreamt he was eating his shoe.
He awoke in the night
In a terrible fright,
And found it was perfectly true!

Humpty Dumpty sat on the wall.
Humpty Dumpty had a great fall.
All the King's horses and all the King's men
Came and had egg salad.

It's All in the Family

SONNY: My brother fell from a fifty-foot tree this morning.
FRIEND: Was he hurt much?
SONNY: No, he had only climbed up about four feet.

NEPHEW: My uncle has a wooden leg and it hurts him a lot.
FRIEND: How can a wooden leg hurt?
NEPHEW: His wife hit him on the head with it.

Mother, is it correct to say you water a horse when he's thirsty?

Yes.

Then, said the boy picking up a saucer, I'm going to milk the cat.

A little boy showed his father a new penknife he found in the street.

"Are you sure it was lost?" asked his father.

"Of course, it was lost. I saw the man looking for it."

A father wrote to the weather bureau and said, "I thought you'd be interested in knowing that I shoveled three feet of 'partly cloudy' from my front steps this morning."

SON: I bet I can make you say "black." What are the colors of the flag?
FATHER: Red, white, and blue.
SON: I told you that I could make you say "black."
FATHER: That's not black.

Have you ever seen a man run over himself? I asked my father if he wanted me to go across the street and get his newspaper and he said he'd rather "run over himself."

GRANDPA: Kids don't walk anywhere any more. Sonny wants to run away from home and Mother says, "Wait, I'll drive you."

FATHER: Did you catch those fish all by yourself?
SON: No, some worms helped me.

DOCTOR: Nobody lives forever.
FATHER: Do you mind if I try?

FRIEND: Do you think anyone can tell the future with cards?
JUNIOR: My mother can. She took one look at my report card and told me exactly what would happen when Dad got home.

MOTHER: Remember that unbreakable toy you gave Mary yesterday?
FATHER: Don't tell me she's broken it already?
MOTHER: No, but she's broken all her other toys with it.

UNCLE: Where's Bill?
NEPHEW: Well, if the ice is as thick as he thinks it is, he's skating. But if it's as thin as I think it is, he's swimming.

A man was trying to teach his wife to drive and she was very nervous. All at once she screamed, "What do I do? Here comes a telephone pole!"

FATHER: Is this a good lake for fish?
FISHERMAN: It must be. I can't get any of them to come out.

Papa Tomato, Mama Tomato, and Baby Tomato went for a walk. Baby Tomato lagged behind so Papa Tomato yelled, "Catch up!"

MOTHER: How did you do on your first day of school?
TOMMY: Not so well, I guess. I have to go back tomorrow.

FATHER: Son, how did you do on your tests today?
SON: O.K., but on one I was like Washington and Lincoln.
FATHER: How was that?
SON: I went down in history.

FATHER: This coffee tastes like mud.
MOTHER: Well, it was ground this morning.

MOTHER: It is important for everyone to go to the dentist twice a year even though it's "boring."

SON: Dad, is it bad luck to have a black cat follow you?
DAD: It depends on whether you're a man or a mouse.

FRIEND: Does your sister know much about cars?
BROTHER: No, she thinks you cool the motor by stripping the gears.

BROTHER: Why did the woman buy glasses with square bottoms instead of round ones?
SISTER: I don't know, why?
BROTHER: So they wouldn't make rings on the table.

SONNY: What did the big firecracker say to the little firecracker?
FRIEND: What?
SONNY: "My Pop is bigger than yours."

Did you ever hear of a person turning into something else?

Well, my big brother was driving Dad's car and he turned into a telephone pole.

FATHER: I wasn't made to be a gardener.
NEIGHBOR: What do you grow in your garden?
FATHER: Tired!

DAD: What are you studying in school these days, Linda?
LINDA: Mostly Gozinta, Daddy.
DAD: What on earth is Gozinta? A new language?
LINDA: No, just Gozinta. Two gozinta 4, 4 gozinta 8, 8 gozinta . . .

A mother was trying to drive her car out of a parking space. First she bumped the car behind, then she scraped the car in front, and when she pulled out, crashed right into a truck. A policeman came up and demanded to see her license. "Don't be silly, officer," she said, "who'd ever give me a license!"

FATHER: How do you stand in school, Jimmy?
JIMMY: Right in the corner, as usual.

BROTHER: The tornado that blew my family's car away left another in its place.
FRIEND: Must have been a trade wind.

MOTHER: Why do Brother's kites fly higher than any others?
SISTER: Because he makes them of flypaper.

Sonny came home after Christmas vacation with a bad report card. His mother said, "Oh my, what was the trouble?"

Sonny answered, "No trouble, you know how things are always marked down after the holidays."

Father went to see his doctor complaining of an itchy elbow. After a long examination, the doctor asked, "Have you ever had this before?"

"Yes," replied Father.

"Well," said the doctor, "it looks like you've got it again."

Junior came home with a new sports car and was greeted by his farmer uncle. "What do you think of it?" asked Junior.

The uncle replied, "Picked it before it was ripe, didn't you?"

MOTHER: What is the best way to keep water from coming in the house?
FATHER: Don't pay the water bill.

Classroom Capers

BRIAN: Why did Robby eat a dollar?
JOHN: I don't know. Why?
BRIAN: It was his lunch money.

TEACHER: Tommy, give me a sentence using the word "camphor."
TOMMY: I was at camp for a week last summer.

TEACHER: Who wrote, "Oh, say can you see?"
MARY: An eye doctor.

A little boy arrived at school and explained that he had been absent because of Egyptian flu—he caught it from his mummy.

TEACHER: Who invented gunpowder?
RICHARD: A lady that wanted guns to look pretty.

TEACHER: If I cut a beefsteak in two, then cut the halves
    in two, what do I get?
PUPIL: Quarters.
TEACHER: And then if I cut it again?
PUPIL: Eighths.
TEACHER: Correct—and cut it again?
PUPIL: Sixteenths.
TEACHER: And again?
PUPIL: Hamburger!

TEACHER: Frederick, you should be ashamed. When I was
    your age I could name all the Presidents.
FREDERICK: Yes, but there were only three or four then.

TEACHER: Let's talk about the grizzly bear. Do we get fur
    from him?
PUPIL: Personally, I'd get as fur from him as possible.

LIBRARIAN: Shhhh, the people next to you can't read.
PUPIL: What a shame! I've been reading since I was six.

TEACHER: Name something beginning with the letter *m*
    which you need to make mayonnaise?
KATHY: Mother.

TEACHER: I asked you to draw a horse and wagon but you've drawn only a horse.
PUPIL: I figured the horse would draw the wagon.

TEACHER: Do you like to come to school, David?
DAVID: Sure, and I like to go home too. It's the in-between time that gets me.

TEACHER: How many sides has a box?
NANCY: Two, inside and outside.

The class was having a composition lesson and the teacher said, "Do not imitate what other people write. Just be yourself and write what's in you."

Tommy turned in the following: "In me there's my stomach, heart, liver, two apples, a piece of pie, and a lemon drop."

TEACHER: What can you tell me about a glacier?
PUPIL: That's the man who puts in the new glass when you have a broken window.

TEACHER: Correct this sentence: "The bull and the cow is in the field."
STEVE: "The cow and the bull is in the field"—ladies come first.

TEACHER IN GEOGRAPHY CLASS: Locate the city of Chicago.
PUPIL: Nearly at the bottom of Lake Michigan.

TEACHER: Where are the kings of England crowned?
JANIE: On their heads.

TEACHER: Name the four seasons.
DANNY: Salt, pepper, mustard, vinegar.

TEACHER: What can you tell me about the Norwegian fiords?
PHILIP: I'm not sure, but they probably get twenty miles to the gallon.

TEACHER: Where was the Declaration of Independence signed?
JERRY: At the bottom.

FIRST PUPIL: If I don't pass this exam, I'll kill myself.
SECOND PUPIL: Why bother? You're dead from the neck up anyway.

GEORGE: It's going to be tough sledding around school tomorrow.
JOHN: Why?
GEORGE: No snow.

TEACHER, ANSWERING THE PHONE: You say Billy has a cold and can't come to school? Who is this speaking?
HOARSE VOICE: This is my father.

TEACHER: How many fingers have you?
JEAN: Ten.
TEACHER: Well, if four were missing, what would you have then?
JEAN: No piano lessons.

TEACHER: What is the plural of "man"?
DUSTY: "Men."
TEACHER: What is the plural of "child"?
DUSTY: "Twins."

TEACHER: What is a mayor?
ANNIE: A mayor is a she horse.

TEACHER: Name three kinds of blood vessels.
PUPIL: Arteries, veins, caterpillars.

TEACHER: You can't sleep in my class.
PUPIL: I could if you didn't talk so loud.

TEACHER: What is a comet?
DEBBIE: A star with a tail.
TEACHER: Good, name one.
DEBBIE: Lassie.

TEACHER: What is a mountain pass?
PUPIL: A mountain pass is a pass given by railroads to their workers so that they can spend their vacations in the mountains.

After discussing the weather peculiarities of March, the teacher asked, "What is it that comes in like a lion and goes out like a lamb?"

THIRD GRADER: Father.

A teacher had given her second graders a lesson on magnets. Later she asked, "My name starts with *m* and I pick up things. What am I?"

They answered, "Mother."

FIRST PUPIL: This school must be haunted.
SECOND PUPIL: Why?
FIRST PUPIL: People are always talking about the school
   spirit.

A teacher asked for sentences using the word "beans."
One pupil wrote: My father grows beans.
              My mother cooks beans.
              We are all human beans.

TEACHER: Give me a sentence using the word "fascinate."
SANDY: I have nine buttons but I can only fasten eight.

TEACHER: What happened in 1809?
TEDDY: Lincoln was born.
TEACHER: Now, what happened in 1812?
TEDDY: He had his third birthday.

TEACHER: Donald, did your father write this story?
DONALD: He started it, but Mother had to do it over.

TEACHER: Do you know what "climate" means?
JENNY: That's what most boys do when they see a ladder.

JUNIOR: I just put a stick of dynamite under the teacher's
   chair.
MOTHER: That's terrible. You go back to the school im-
   mediately!
JUNIOR: What school?

TEACHER: Children, there will be only a half day of school this morning.

PUPILS: Whoopee! Hooray! Yippee!

TEACHER: We will have the other half this afternoon.

Why do kindergarten teachers enjoy life?
Because they make the little things count.

TEACHER: Correct this sentence: "It was me who broke the window."

PETER: "It wasn't me who broke the window."

FATHER: Why were you kept after school on the very first day?

SON: I didn't know where the Azores were.

FATHER: Well, in the future remember where you put things.

What's the difference between a pen and a pencil?
You push a pen and a pencil has to be led.

SHAMUS: What did the alligator say when he had a lot of homework?

ELIZABETH: What?

SHAMUS: I'm swamped.

TEACHER: Why does the Statue of Liberty stand in New York harbor?

TEDDY: Because it can't sit down.

TEACHER: Why was it said that "the sun never sets on the British Empire"?

PUPIL: Because the British Empire is in the east and the sun sets in the west.

PUPIL: My dog knows arithmetic.

TEACHER: Really?

PUPIL: Yes, ask him what 16 minus 16 is and he'll say nothing.

TEACHER: Tommy, how did you get that swelling on your nose?

TOMMY: I bent to smell a brose in my garden.

TEACHER: There's no b in "rose."

TOMMY: There was in this one!

TEACHER: Spell Mississippi for me, Jimmy.

JIMMY: Which one, the river or the state?

TEACHER: I don't see how one person can make so many mistakes on his homework!

ALFIE: It wasn't one person. My dad helped me.

TEACHER: Where were you this morning, Mickey?

MICKEY: At the dentist.

TEACHER: You must be feeling better now.

MICKEY: I sure do—he wasn't there!

TEACHER: Do you know what they call an Indian reservation?
JERRY: The home of the brave.

FIRST PUPIL: What's big, purple, and lies across the sea from us?
SMARTY: Grape Britain.

BILLY: What was my name in first grade?
TEACHER: Billy.
BILLY: In second grade?
TEACHER: Billy.
BILLY: Knock, knock.
TEACHER: Who's there?
BILLY: Billy.
TEACHER: Billy who?
BILLY: Don't tell me you forgot my name so soon.

TEACHER: Who can tell me what a myth is?
JENNY: A female moth.

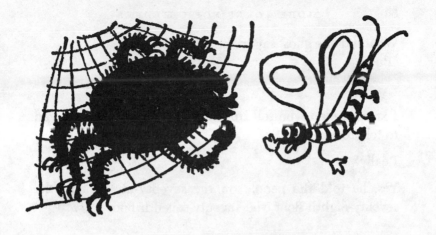

Gruesomes

Hey, Mom, why am I walking around in circles?
Be quiet, Junior, or I'll nail your other foot to the floor!

Why did the man put his foot on the stove?
He wanted to pop his corns.

My brother is working with two thousand men under him.
Really. What does he do?
He cuts the grass in a cemetery.

My brother has a broken arm because the doctor told him
to follow a prescription for a cold.

How did he break his arm?

The prescription flew out the window and he jumped out
after it.

What did one ghost say to the other ghost?
"Boo!"

I know a man who fell from the eightieth floor and lived to tell about it.

Really?

Yes, he told the people on the seventy-ninth floor, the seventy-eighth floor, the seventy-seventh floor . . .

What animal is a cannibal?
A cow. It eats its fodder.

What would you find if you put your finger in Johnson's ear?

Johnson's wax.

What is green, lies in a ditch, and is covered with cooky crumbs?

A girl scout who has fainted.

Did you hear about the pilot who believed in terra firma?
The firmer the ground the less the terror.

If a man smashes a clock, he can be accused of killing time, unless the clock struck first.

How do you keep a fish from smelling?
Cut off his nose.

FIRST CANNIBAL: I don't care for your friend.
SECOND CANNIBAL: O.K., just eat the vegetables.

Why did the man put garbage in his shoes?
Because he wanted to feed his piggies.

What has four legs and flies?
A dead horse.

The remedy for a bad liver?
Take it back to the butcher.

What are Baby Monster's parents called?
Dead and Mummy.

"Look here," complained a man to his neighbor, "you've got to make your dog stop chasing all the sportscars that drive down our street."

"I can't do much about that," answered the man. "Most dogs chase cars."

"Yes, but your dog catches them and buries them in my back yard."

I was operated on last week and laughed all through the operation.

Why?

The doctor had me in stitches.

Why did the little cannibal get expelled from school?
He got caught buttering up the teacher.

WAITER: These are the best eggs we've had for years.
MAN: I'd rather have some you've only had a few days.

Who has the most friends for lunch?
A cannibal.

CUSTOMER: Why did it take you so long with just half a broiled chicken?
WAITER: We couldn't kill half a chicken and had to wait for someone to order the other half.

What did one tooth say to the other tooth?
"The dentist's taking me out tonight."

Why do surgeons wear masks during an operation?

So that if anyone makes a mistake, they won't know who did it.

MOTHER AT THE DENTIST'S: Now, Bobby, be a good boy and say "Ah" so the doctor can get his finger out of your mouth.

What has eighteen legs, nine eyes, and twenty-one ears?

I don't know, but I wouldn't like to see it crawling up my arm!

PATIENT: Doctor, I'm scared to death! This is my first operation!
DOCTOR: I know just how you feel. You're my first patient!

What do witches eat for dinner?
Halloweenies.

CUSTOMER: This steak is awful. How was it cooked?
WAITER: It was smothered in onions, sir.
CUSTOMER: Well, it sure died a hard death!

Did you hear about the fellow who fell into the lens grinder and made a spectacle of himself?

MAN: Is there any stew on the menu?
WAITER: No. There was, but I wiped it off.

PATIENT: Why do you whistle when you operate, Doctor?
DOCTOR: It helps take my mind off my work.

"Waiter," exclaimed the angry diner, "you've got your thumb on my steak!"

"Yes," said the waiter. "I don't want it to fall on the floor again."

What did the mother ghost say to the baby ghost?
"Don't spook until spooken to."

A Peace Corps worker was sent to a cannibal tribe. When the chief was asked what was learned, he said, "We had a slight taste of democracy."

DOCTOR: What seems to be your trouble?
PATIENT: I have trouble breathing.
DOCTOR: Here's something to stop that.

The Happy Joker

NEIGHBOR: Why are you painting your house all bundled
up like that?
JOKER: Well, it says on the paint can to be sure to put on
three coats.

What do you get when you cross a pig and a centipede?
Bacon and legs.

A man walked into a clothing store. "What can I do for
you, sir?" asked a clerk.

"I'd like to try on that suit in the window," the man
answered.

"Well, sir," said the clerk, "we'd rather you'd use the dressing room."

JOHNNY: Look, Mother, here is a green snake!
MOTHER: Leave it alone. It's probably just as dangerous as a ripe one.

Why did the joker make his dog sit in the sun?
He wanted to have a hot dog.

FRIEND: Why did you paste a calendar on your eyeglasses?
JOKER: So I can gaze into the future.

Why did the joker throw butter out the window?
He wanted to see the butterfly.

RANCHER: What kind of a saddle do you want—with or without a horn?
DOPEY DUDE: Without, I guess. There doesn't seem to be much traffic around here.

Did you hear about the joker who stayed up all night to see where the sun went? Finally it dawned on him.

Why did the joker put his radio in the refrigerator?
He wanted to hear cool music.

BOSS: Why are you here? Didn't you receive my letter saying that you're fired?
JOKER: Yes, but on the envelope it said, "Return after five days."

DRIVING INSTRUCTOR: Now, when there's an emergency you must put on the brake.
JOKER: Why? I thought that came with the car.

Why did the joker get kicked out of the submarine service?

He liked to sleep with the windows open.

FRIEND: Is it good manners to eat fried chicken with your fingers?
JOKER: No, you should eat the fingers separately.

Why did the joker take a hammer to bed with him?
He wanted to hit the hay.

Why did the joker close his eyes when he passed the refrigerator?

Because he didn't want to see the salad dressing.

FRIEND: Ouch! That water is so hot it burned my hand!
JOKER: Serves you right. You should have felt it before you
put your hand in it.

WAITER: Would you like black coffee, sir?
JOKER: What other colors do you have?

Why did the joker hang a bell around the neck of his
bull?

In case his horns didn't work.

FRIEND: I had the TV on last night.
JOKER: Did it fit?

POLICEMAN: Didn't you see that arrow?
JOKER: Man, I didn't even see the Indian!

Why did the joker from Louisiana call himself Tex?
He didn't want to be called Louise.

JOKER: Oh my, I've been stung by a wasp!
FRIEND: Quick, put something on it.
JOKER: I can't. It flew away.

FRIEND: Will you join me in a bowl of soup?
JOKER: Do you think there's room for both of us?

Why did the joker eat yeast and drink shoe polish?
He wanted to rise and shine.

MECHANIC: I've found the trouble with your car. You have
a short circuit in the wiring.
JOKER: Well, why don't you lengthen it?

Why did the joker saw off the legs of the stove?
The recipe said to use a low flame.

MOTHER: Don't go in the water right after dinner. It's
dangerous to swim on a full stomach.
JOKER: That's all right. I'll swim on my back.

Why did the joker feed dollar bills to his horse?
He wanted to have a bucking bronco.

FRIEND: Do you like codfish balls?
JOKER: I don't know. I've never been to one.

FRIEND: Can you stand on your head?
JOKER: No, I can't step that high.

EYE DOCTOR: Have your eyes ever been checked?
JOKER: No, they've always been brown.

JOKER: The doctor told me to drink carrot juice after a
    hot bath.
FRIEND: How does carrot juice taste?
JOKER: I don't know yet. I'm still drinking the hot bath.

Why did the joker put on a wet shirt?
Because the label said, "Wash and wear."

FRIEND: What would you do if you broke your arm in two
    places?
JOKER: I wouldn't go to those two places any more.

Why did the joker throw his pants out the window?
Because he heard the newsboy call, "Free press."

FRIEND: How did you break your leg?
JOKER: I put a cigarette in an open manhole and stepped
on it.

Why did the joker cut a hole in the rug?
To see the floor show.

Bugs, Birds, and Others

What do they call a monkey that sells potato chips?
A chip monk.

Can you spell "blind pig" with two letters?
P g—pig without an eye.

Why does a hen lay eggs?
Because if she dropped them, they'd break.

What's black and white and red all over?
A sunburned zebra.

Every dog has its day, but a dog with a broken tail has a weak end.

What happens to a deer when an archer shoots at it and misses?

It has an arrow escape.

Why did the farmer call his pig Ink?
Because he was always running out of the pen.

If a rooster lays one egg on a roof, which side will it fall off?

Neither, a rooster can't lay eggs.

Papa Lightning Bug said to Mama Lightning Bug, "Isn't Junior bright for his age!"

Did you know that all the animals went to Noah's Ark in pairs?

Yes, except the worms. They came in apples.

I have a friend who goes to bed with his shoes on.
Who's that?
My horse.

Name four animals of the cat family.
The father cat, the mother cat, and two kittens.

What's worse than raining cats and dogs?
I don't know unless maybe hailing buses.

Why can't a duck fly upside down?
Because he would quack up.

If eight sparrows are on a roof and you shoot one, how many remain?

One, the one you shot. The rest fly away.

When is a shaggy dog most likely to enter a house?
When the door is open.

Why is a dog's tail like the heart of a tree?
Because it's farthest from the bark.

PATIENT: What is the best way to avoid infection caused by biting insects?
DOCTOR: Don't bite any.

My cousin swallowed a frog.
Did it make him sick?
Yes, he's liable to croak any minute.

Girl: Say, your dog bit me on the ankle.
Boy: Well, that's as high as he could reach.

A donkey seeing a zebra for the first time said to himself, "Imagine that! A donkey who has been in jail."

What does a hen do when it stands on one leg?
Lifts up the other leg.

What part of a fish weighs the most?
The scales.

The reason a stork stands on one foot: if he lifted the other one, he'd fall down.

What does a calf become after it is one year old?
Two years old.

What's the name of your dog?
Ginger.
Does Ginger bite?
No, Ginger snaps.

Did you hear about the dog that went to the flea circus?
No, what happened?
He stole the show.

If bananas come under fruit and carrots come under vegetables, what does an egg come under?

A chicken.

Did you hear about the horse who ate an electric wire?
He went haywire.

If there are four sheep, two dogs, and one herdsman, how
many feet are there?

Twenty-six?

No, only two. Sheep have hoofs, dogs have paws, and so
one man has two feet.

What would you have if you crossed a flea with a rabbit?
A bug's bunny.

Why are four-legged animals poor dancers?
Because they have two left feet.

What's gray, has four legs, and a trunk?
A mouse going on a trip.

When is a farmer like a magician?
When he turns his cow into the pasture.

Seven cows were walking along single file. Which one turned around and said, "I see six pairs of horns"?

The first cow.

Wrong. Cows can't talk.

Why is a hen sitting on a fence like a penny?
That's easy. The head's on one side and the tail's on the other.

Why does a rabbit like diamonds?
They're measured in carrots.

CUSTOMER: Do you have alligator shoes?
CLERK: Yes, sir. What size does your alligator wear?

What creature eats the least?
A moth. It just eats holes.

Why are fish smart?
Because they travel in schools.

What did the baby chicken say when it saw the orange in the mother's nest?

"Look at the orange Mama laid."

Where does a sheep get his hair cut?
At a baa-baa shop.

Why did the chicken stop halfway across the road?
She wanted to lay it on the line.

What animal can jump higher than a house?
Any animal—a house can't jump.

What do you call a dog with a watch?
A watchdog.

What is a dog without a tail?
It's a hot dog.

What do you call a cat who drinks lemonade?
A sourpuss.

A boo-bee bird is a small bird that flies into beehives and says, "Boo, bee!"

Why is a lollipop like a race horse?
The more you lick it the faster it goes.

What's the difference between a cat and a frog?
A cat has nine lives and a frog croaks every night.

Two ducks were walking through the park in a snowstorm. The duck on the right was limping. Why?

He had a rock in his galoshes.

Do you know what the fellow did who found a horse in the bathtub?

Pulled the plug out.

Why does the rabbit have a very shiny nose?
Cause the powder puff is at the other end.

Name six animals from the Arctic region?
Three bears and three seals.

Is man an animal?

Yes, man is an animal who is split halfway up and walks on the split end.

How can you prove that a horse has six legs?
He has fore (four) legs in front and two behind.

What's black and yellow and goes "zub, zub, zub"?
A bee flying backwards.

Why is the barn so noisy?
The cows have horns.

Did you ever tickle a mule?
No, why?
You should try it. You'll get a big kick out of it.

Why are carrots good for your eyes?
You never saw a rabbit wearing glasses, did you?

FARM BOY: My father doesn't know whether to get a cow or a tractor.
CITY BOY: He'd sure look funny trying to ride a cow.
FARM BOY: He'd look even funnier trying to milk a tractor.

What do they call a smart duck in school?
A wise quacker.

Did you hear about the man who crossed a bumblebee
with a doorbell and got a humdinger?

What bird is a letter?
Jay.

What bird can lift heavy weights?
A crane.

What bird is found anywhere in the world, has wings, but
can't fly.

A dead bird.

What bird is present at every meal?
A swallow.

What is the gloomiest bird?
A bluebird.

What bird is the most impudent?
A mockingbird.

What kind of bird is like a car?
A goose—they both honk.

What is a bull called when it is sleeping?
A bulldozer.

What has six legs, a tail, and two heads?
A lady riding a horse.

What mother loves to see her children go to the dogs?
A mother flea.

Why do hummingbirds always hum?
Because they don't know the words to the song.

What do squirrels have that no other animal has?
Little squirrels.

Why can't a frog talk?
He's got a man in his throat.

Why do people say a chicken has no sense of humor?
Because all its yolks are the same.

What did the mother pigeon say to her baby?
"Please stop walking people-toed."

Who's never hungry at Thanksgiving dinner?
The Turkey—he's always stuffed.

How do you keep a skunk from smelling?
Hold his nose.

Why do little pigs eat so much?
They like to make hogs of themselves.

What ant lives in a house?
An occupant.

What's the difference between a tired little-league pitcher
and his tired dog?

The boy wears a whole uniform and the dog only pants.

Every time Bertha practiced the violin her dog howled and howled. Finally a neighbor called and said, "Couldn't Bertha play some tune the dog doesn't know?"

What animals need to be oiled?
Mice—they squeak.

Why is a porcupine so nervous?
Because he is on pins and needles.

What grows up while it grows down?
A baby duckling.

If there were seven copycats on a wall and one jumped off, how many would be left?
None.

Did you know that it takes three sheep to make a sweater?
No, I didn't even know they could knit.

How many hairs in a rabbit's tail?
None. They are all outside.

I've got the smartest cat!

How come?

It eats cheese and then waits at a mousehole with baited breath.

What animal eats with its tail?
They all do. They can't take them off.

What is a three-letter word that is a mousetrap?
"Cat."

Why are you sitting on this telephone pole, Mrs. Crow?
Because I'm making a long-distance caw.

A boy from the city was visiting his country cousin. He spotted some milk bottles in the yard and said, "Look! I found a cow's nest!"

Dinosaurs, Elephants, Etc.

Why did the elephants quit the circus?
They got tired of working for peanuts.

What do you do with old bowling balls?
Give them to the elephants to shoot marbles.

How does one dinosaur tell another to hurry up?
"Pronto, Saurus!"

Why did the elephant have holes in his hide?
He forgot to put mothballs in his trunk.

What is the difference between a flea and an elephant?
A flea can't have an elephant but an elephant can have fleas.

Why did the elephant wear a green suit?
To hide in the grass.

I went to the zoo today and I saw a camel with eight feet.
How could that be?
There were two of them.

How can you tell if an elephant has been in your refrigerator?

From his footprints in the jelly.

Why is a hippopotamus like a robin?
Because neither can ride a bicycle.

I know of a baby that gained twenty pounds on elephant's milk.

That's amazing. Whose baby?

The elephant's.

What did one duck-billed dinosaur say to the other duck-billed dinosaur when they wanted to leave the party?

"Let's duck, Bill."

What's the difference between an elephant and a jar of peanut butter?

The elephant doesn't stick to the roof of your mouth.

Do you know why the elephant wears dark glasses?

If you had all those jokes told about you, you wouldn't want to be recognized either.

Why did the elephant lie in the middle of the sidewalk?
To trip the ants.

What did the dinosaur say when he saw his first kangaroo?
Look at that kooky leaping cousin!

Why do elephants have trunks?
Because they don't have glove compartments.

What did the elephant say to the platypus?

"I never forget a face but with yours I'll make an exception."

Why do dragons sleep in the daytime?
So they can hunt knights.

What did one strong dinosaur say to the other on their way to the swimming hole?

"Let's pool our strength."

What is worse than a giraffe with a sore throat?
An elephant with a cold.

Why does an elephant climb up a cherry tree?
Because he's silly.

What do you call it if nine elephants wear pink sneakers and one elephant wears blue?

Nine out of ten elephants wear pink sneakers.

What time is it when an elephant sits on a fence?
Time to buy a new fence.

Why did the elephant paint himself all different colors?
So he could hide in a package of M&M's.

What does a dinosaur call a Brontosaurus?
Prehistoric.

What kind of gun do you use to shoot a purple elephant?

A purple elephant gun.

What kind of gun do you use to shoot a red elephant?

A red elephant gun.

No. You squeeze the elephant till he turns purple and then shoot him with a purple elephant gun.

Why aren't elephants allowed on the beach?
Because they can't keep their trunks up.

Why is a snake so smart?
Because you can't pull his leg.

Why did the dinosaur stare at his footprints in the sand?
He wondered if he was coming or going.

Why does an elephant sit on a marshmallow?
To keep from falling into the cocoa.

How many lions can you put in an empty cage?
One. After that the cage is not empty.

How do you stop a lion from charging?
Take away his credit card.

Why does a mother kangaroo hate rainy days?
Because then the children have to play inside.

What should you do when you see a lion?
Hope to goodness he doesn't see you.

How come giraffes have such small appetites?
With them a little goes a long way.

What did the grape say when the elephant stepped on it?
Nothing, it just let out a little whine.

How do you fit five elephants in a Volkswagen?
Two in the front, two in the back, and one in the glove compartment.

What does an elephant call a dinosaur?
Extinct.

What is as big as a dinosaur and doesn't weigh an ounce?
A dinosaur's shadow.

Why did the elephant paint her head yellow?
She wanted to see if blondes had more fun.

What is red, white, and gray?
A can of elephant gumbo soup.

VETERINARIAN: What's the trouble?
KANGAROO: It's just that I haven't been feeling jumpy lately.

What did the angry little dinosaur shout at the big dinosaur who wouldn't play with him?

"You old fossil!"

What did the boy octopus say to the girl octopus?

I want to hold your hand hand hand hand hand hand hand hand.

What's gray on the inside and clear on the outside?
An elephant in a Baggie.

Why did the elephant lie upside down in the middle of the road with his feet in the air?
He wanted to trip the birds.

Did you hear about the rich dinosaur who had a large statue of a gas station attendant on his front lawn?

How is an elephant like a Volkswagen?
The trunk is in front.

Why does a dinosaur sit on his hind legs?
If he didn't, he'd be standing up!

Calvin

AUNTIE: What's the difference between a hippopotamus
    and a piece of paper?
CALVIN: You can't make a spitball out of a hippopotamus.

CALVIN: Ask me if I'm a tiger.
COUSIN: Are you a tiger?
CALVIN: Yup. Ask me if I'm a rabbit.
COUSIN: Are you a rabbit?
CALVIN: No, I just told you I'm a tiger.

FRIENDLY STRANGER TO CALVIN ON THE BEACH: My, aren't
    you tan from the sun.
CALVIN: No, I'm Calvin Smith from the earth.

CALVIN: I was named after Abe Lincoln.

FRIEND: Then your name is really Abraham?

CALVIN: Nope, it's Calvin.

FRIEND: But you just said you were named after Abraham Lincoln.

CALVIN: Yes, he was named in 1809 and I was named in 1975.

MOTHER: Boys, what's this argument about?

CALVIN: Oh, there's no argument. Bobby thinks I'm not going to give him half my candy and I think the same.

CALVIN: The typewriter is broken.

FATHER: What's the matter with it?

CALVIN: It can't spell.

MOTHER: Aren't you going to straighten up your room?

CALVIN: Why? Is it crooked?

UNCLE: Were you hurt when you were on the football team?

CALVIN: No, it was when the football team was on me!

CALVIN TO FRIEND: Mother says my fourteen-year-old sister is going to have an operation to have the telephone removed from her mouth.

NEIGHBOR: Did you break your arm?
CALVIN: No, just the bone in it.

SISTER: Ask mom if we can go to the movies.
CALVIN: You ask her. You've known her longer than I have.

MOTHER: Wash your hands for dinner.
CALVIN: They aren't really dirty—just kinda blurred.

MOTHER: What's your brother crying about? Didn't I tell
    you to give him anything he wanted?
CALVIN: Yes, Mother, but I've dug him a hole and now he
    wants me to bring it in the house.

A fat lady stepped on the scales, not knowing they were
out of order. The arrow stopped at seventy-five pounds.

"Wow," exclaimed Calvin, who was watching. "She's hol-
low!"

CALVIN AFTER HIS FIRST HORSEBACK RIDE: I never knew any-
    thing filled with hay could feel so hard.

MOTHER AT THE CIRCUS: Calvin, what are you doing?
CALVIN: I'm feeding half my peanuts to the monkeys.
MOTHER: That's nice.
CALVIN: Sure, I'm giving them the shells.

FATHER: Calvin, how did you get so dirty?
CALVIN: I'm closer to the ground than you are.

AUNTIE: What is the hardest thing about learning to ride a bike?
CALVIN: The pavement.

TEACHER: What is your new brother's name?
CALVIN: I don't know yet. I can't understand a word he says.

After much urging from his mother, Calvin wrote the following thank-you note to his aunt: "Thank you for your nice present. I always wanted a pincushion, although not very much."

CALVIN: Mom, I just took a splinter out of my hand with a pin.
MOTHER: A pin! Don't you know that's dangerous?
CALVIN: Oh no, I used a safety pin.

FATHER: How did you get that scratch on your forehead?
CALVIN: I bit myself.
FATHER: How could you bite yourself on the forehead?
CALVIN: I stood on a chair.

UNCLE: Calvin, what are you going to give your little
brother for Christmas this year?

CALVIN: I don't know yet. Last year I gave him the
measles.

NEIGHBOR: Has your new baby learned to talk yet?

CALVIN: Oh yes, we're teaching him to keep quiet now.

FRIEND: Why are you jumping up and down?

CALVIN: I just took some medicine and it says, "Shake
well."

MOTHER: Why are you standing in front of the mirror with
your eyes closed?

CALVIN: I want to see what I look like when I'm asleep.

DENTIST: What kind of filling do you want in your tooth?

CALVIN: Chocolate.

CALVIN (LOST ON A SHOPPING TRIP) TO POLICEMAN: Did you
see a mother going by without me?

MOTHER: Calvin, shoo those flies.

CALVIN: What size do they take?

CALVIN: Will I have to eat my cake with a fork when company comes?

MOTHER: Certainly.

CALVIN: Then may I have another piece to practice on?

FRIEND: What do you think of the new boy?

CALVIN: He's so dumb he flunked sandbox when he was in kindergarten.

FATHER: Do you know what "transparent" means?

CALVIN: "Transparent" means something you can see through—like a keyhole.

MOTHER: It's time for dinner, Calvin. Go wash your hands.

CALVIN: Do I have to wash both of them?

MOTHER: No, just one, if you can.

POLICEMAN TO CALVIN WITH SUITCASE: Where are you going?

CALVIN: Running away.

POLICEMAN: But I've watched you and all you do is keep going around the block.

CALVIN: I'm not allowed to cross the street by myself.

Calvin was paying his first visit to a church that had choir-boys dressed in white robes and said, "Are all those fellows going to get a haircut?"

MOTHER: Why do you want to keep this bag of dirt, Calvin?

CALVIN: It's instant mudpie mix.

MOTHER: Calvin, stop all that jumping around and just take your medicine.

CALVIN: But it says to take it two nights running and skip a night.

Daffy Definitions

What is a bluebell?
A moody beauty.

Define "pasteurize."
Too far to see.

A mountain range is a cooking stove made specially for use at high altitudes.

The Eskimos are God's frozen people.

A sure-footed man is a man who when he kicks you does not miss.

What is an octopus?
An eight-sided cat.

Etiquette is yawning with your mouth closed.

A duck is a chicken on snowshoes.

An icicle is an eavesdropper.

A humbug is a bug that can't sing.

An undercover agent is a spy in bed.

A stagecoach is a drama teacher.

Bulletin?
I've been shot!

Shish kebab is what you say to Kebab when you want him to be quiet.

"Intense" is where the boy scouts sleep.

A ski tow is a bug that bites.

"Hunter" is what the man told his dog when he wanted to find his daughter.

Hatchet is what a hen does to an egg.

Sea shell is a torpedo.

Define a circle.
A circle is a round line with no kinks in it, joined up so as not to show where it began.

Engineer?
Train coming.

What tree is the sweetest?   Maple.
What tree will keep you warm?   Fir.
What tree is near the sea?   Beech.
What is the calendar tree?   Date.
What is the double tree?   Pear.

Depress is the thing you print newspapers on.

Hot rod—a branding iron.

A lunatic is a small bloodsucking insect that lives on the moon.

Cartoon is music to drive by.

Pussywillow is a cat's IOU.

Southpaw is a daddy in Dixie.

Contents—prison-camp shelters.

A dog kennel is a barking lot.

A maestro is a leader of a mouse band.

What is a daffy-down-dilly?
A crazy, mixed-up pickle.

Migraine?
The wheat is mine.

Infantry is a small sapling.

What is a witch doctor's mistake?
A voodoo boo-boo.

Pigeon-toed?
Half pigeon, half toad.

What does "campaign" mean?
When you get hurt at camp.

Gruesome?
A little bit taller.

What is cabbage?
The age of a taxi.

Knock-knocks

GIRL: Knock, knock.
BOY: Who's there?
GIRL: Avenue.
BOY: Avenue who?
GIRL: Avenue heard this knock-knock joke before?

BOY: Knock, knock.
GIRL: Who's there?
BOY: Roach.
GIRL: Roach who?
BOY: Roach you a letter but you didn't answer.

BOY: Knock, knock.
GIRL: Who's there?
BOY: Radio.
GIRL: Radio who?
BOY: Radio not, here I come.

GIRL: Knock, knock.
BOY: Who's there?
GIRL: Sharon.
BOY: Sharon who?
GIRL: Sharon share alike.

BOY: Knock, knock.
GIRL: Who's there?
BOY: Cereal.
GIRL: Cereal who?
BOY: Cereal soon.

BOY: Knock, knock.
GIRL: Who's there?
BOY: Disgust.
GIRL: Disgust who?
BOY: Disgust of wind is strong.

GIRL: Knock, knock.
BOY: Who's there?
GIRL: Crunch.
BOY: Crunch who?
GIRL: God bless you.

BOY: Knock, knock.
GIRL: Who's there?
BOY: Marmalade.
GIRL: Marmalade who?
BOY: "Marmalade me," said the baby chick.

GIRL: Knock, knock.
BOY: Who's there?
GIRL: Henrietta and Juliet.
BOY: Henrietta and Juliet who?
GIRL: Henrietta big dinner and got sick. Juliet the same
thing, but she's O.K.

Boy: Knock, knock.
Girl: Who's there?
Boy: I am.
Girl: I am who?
Boy: You mean you don't know?

Boy: Knock, knock.
Girl: Who's there?
Boy: Idaho.
Girl: Idaho who?
Boy: Idaho your garden if you want me to.

Girl: Kock, knock.
Boy: Who's there?
Girl: Adam.
Boy: Adam who?
Girl: Adam up and tell me how much.

Boy: Knock, knock.
Girl: Who's there?
Boy: Targets.
Girl: Targets who?
Boy: Targets all over my shoes since they fixed the road.

Boy: Knock, knock.
Girl: Who's there?
Boy: Daryl (Darrell).
Girl: Daryl who?
Boy: Daryl never be a better friend than you.

GIRL: Knock, knock.
BOY: Who's there?
GIRL: Beef.
BOY: Beef who?
GIRL: Before I tell you, let me in.

BOY: Knock, knock.
GIRL: Who's there?
BOY: Sarah.
GIRL: Sarah who?
BOY: Sarah doctor in the house?

BOY: Knock, knock.
GIRL: Who's there?
BOY: Althea.
GIRL: Althea who?
BOY: Althea later, alligator.

GIRL: Knock, knock.
BOY: Who's there?
GIRL: Mikey.
BOY: Mikey who?
GIRL: Mikey's stuck in the lock and I can't get it out.

BOY: Knock, knock.
GIRL: Who's there?
BOY: Dwayne.
GIRL: Dwayne who?
BOY: Dwayne the tub, I'm drowning.

GIRL: Knock, knock.
BOY: Who's there?
GIRL: Celeste.
BOY: Celeste who?
GIRL: Celeste time I'm going to tell you to be quiet.

BOY: Knock, knock.
GIRL: Who's there?
BOY: Orange.
GIRL: Orange who?
BOY: Orange you coming out to play?

BOY: Knock, knock.
GIRL: Who's there?
BOY: Cook.
GIRL: Cook who?
BOY: I'm not talking to anyone who's cuckoo.

GIRL: Knock, knock.
BOY: Who's there?
GIRL: Tickum.
BOY: Tickum who?
GIRL: Tickum up, I'm a tongue-tied wobba.

BOY: Knock, knock.
GIRL: Who's there?
BOY: Isabel.
GIRL: Isabel who?
BOY: Isabel ringing?

Boy: Knock, knock.

Girl: Who's there?

Boy: Heaven.

Girl: Heaven who?

Boy: Heaven you heard enough of these knock-knock jokes?